Mustangs

Wild Horses of the American West

Mustangs

Wild Horses of the American West

by Jay Featherly

A Carolrhoda Nature Watch Book

Carolrhoda Books, Inc./Minneapolis

Map on page 8 based on material from
United States Department of the Interior,
Bureau of Land Management

This book is available in two editions:
Library binding by Carolrhoda Books, Inc.
Soft cover by First Avenue Editions
241 First Avenue North
Minneapolis, Minnesota 55401

LIBRARY OF CONGRESS CATALOGING-IN-PUBLICATION DATA

Featherly, Jay.
  Mustangs: wild horses of the American West.

  "A Carolrhoda nature watch book."
  Summary: Describes the habits and behavior of the wild
horses which have roamed across the American West for
hundreds of years.
    1. Wild horses—West (U.S.)—Juvenile literature.
2. Mustang—Juvenile literature. [1. Mustang.
2. Horses] I. Title.
SF360.3.U6F43   1986   599.72'5   86-8314
ISBN 0-87614-293-5 (lib. bdg.)
ISBN 0-87614-450-4 (pbk.)

1 2 3 4 5 6 7 8 9 10 95 94 93 92 91 90 89 88 87 86

Wild horses have roamed the American West for hundreds of years. At one time there were millions of these untamed horses, which are called **mustangs**, living on the lush grasslands with bison, antelope, and other prairie animals.

Where did these mustangs come from? The first "wild" horses were actually tame horses. They were brought to the New World by Spanish explorers who came in search of gold. Some of the Spanish horses probably escaped or were turned loose. These became the first mustangs to roam free. The name *mustang* may come from *mesteño*, the Spanish word for stray animal.

The explorers' horses were the first such animals that the Indians living in the Southwest had ever seen. Soon the Indians began using the horse for hunting and traveling. Eventually, some of the Indians' horses escaped and joined the horses lost by the Spanish.

In the 1840s, when wagon trains of settlers began crossing the Great Plains, different **breeds**, or kinds, of horses broke loose from their owners and ran with the wild horses. Other domestic horses were simply abandoned to live on the prairies. All these horses, together with the Spanish horses, formed the great mustang herds. As time passed, the different breeds of horses **interbred**. This means that the wild horses of today are all **hybrids**, or mixtures, of the original domestic breeds.

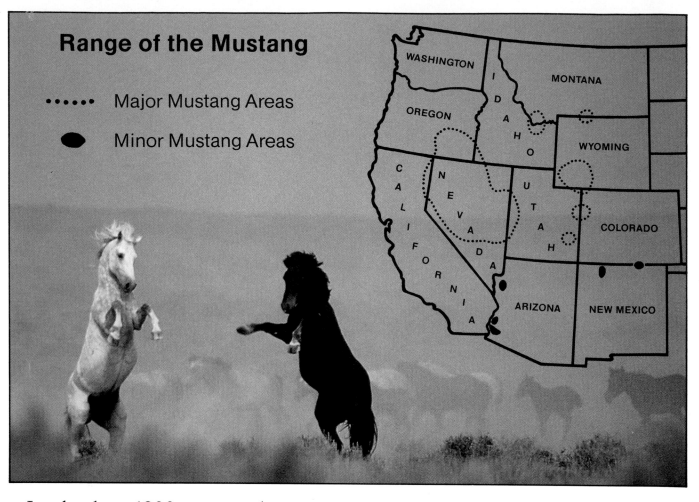

Range of the Mustang

•••••• Major Mustang Areas

● Minor Mustang Areas

WASHINGTON
OREGON
IDAHO
MONTANA
WYOMING
CALIFORNIA
NEVADA
UTAH
COLORADO
ARIZONA
NEW MEXICO

In the late 1800s, more than two million mustangs wandered throughout the West. As ranches and farms spread over the land, the wild horses were captured and killed to make room for livestock and crops. After a while, only a few wild horse herds survived, and they were forced to live in harsh, uninhabited desert country.

By the 1960s, many people worried that the mustangs would soon vanish forever. Thousands of schoolchildren wrote letters to their congressmen asking the government to help save the last wild horses. In 1971, a law was finally passed to protect the mustangs.

Today wild horses band together in a few remote regions of the American West. Most are found in the sagebrush deserts of Nevada and Wyoming, and the rest are scattered throughout eight other western states. About forty thousand wild horses survive today.

Wild horses have adapted well to life on the western deserts. Mustangs are generally smaller than most domestic horses. A Thoroughbred racehorse can weigh 1,200 pounds (544 kg), but a large wild stallion may weigh only 1,000 pounds (454 kg). Mustangs are smaller because they live in a harsh environ-ment. They must work hard to find enough grass to eat each day. With such a meager food supply, young horses in the wild grow slowly. However, if they are captured and raised on a diet of hay and oats, wild foals grow to be as large as domestic horses.

Though mustangs weigh less than domestic horses, they are not weak or sickly. Just to survive, mustangs must be hardier than domestic horses. The harsh living conditions in the wild make them tough and strong. In summer they endure the hot desert sun without any trees to shade them. Each day they travel many miles in the heat to find water. In winter they stand unprotected against fierce blizzards that blow across the open land. After a storm, they have to paw away the snow to reach clumps of frozen grass beneath, and they must break the ice on water holes with their hooves in order to drink.

In such a severe environment, mustangs live up to 20 years. Many domestic horses live longer than that because their owners take special care of them when the animals grow old.

Surrounded by vast, open lands, wild horses are constantly alert to danger. In the past, wolves, mountain lions, and prairie fires often threatened the horses, but today mustangs fear humans more than any other threat.

Wild horses' sharp senses alert them to approaching danger. They often pause

and prick up their ears to listen for unusual sounds. Their sense of smell is keen, and, through their legs, they can feel vibrations in the ground. Mustangs can spot moving objects at long distances, and they can see much better at night than people do. Since mustangs' senses give them an early warning of danger, their normal means of defense, running, is an effective one.

Wild horses live in groups. There are several different kinds of groups in mustang society, the most common of which is the **family band**. It is usually made up of a single **stallion** (an adult male horse) and 1 to 8 **mares** (adult female horses). The stallion has won the mares in battles with other stallions. A very powerful stallion may gather up to 20 mares. The family band also includes **foals** (newborn male or female horses) and young **colts** (male horses under the age of four).

A male that leads a family band is known as a **band stallion** or **dominant stallion**. The mares in a family band are often called the **harem**. Unlike most hoofed mammals, the wild stallion keeps his mares together throughout the year, not just during the breeding season.

Leading a family band is hard work for the fiercely protective band stallion. His biggest responsibility is defending his mares from rival males. These rivals are often waiting nearby to steal any unprotected female, so a dominant stallion must always be alert.

While grazing, he constantly lifts his head to watch for approaching rival stallions. He also circles his band frequently to keep his mares bunched close together. The band stallion almost always sleeps standing up so that he is ready to react in an instant. Other mustangs also doze while standing, but sometimes they lie down on their sides and sleep more deeply.

If a mare or a foal strays from the band, the dominant stallion quickly herds it back to rejoin the other horses. He signals this command by lowering his head and flattening back his ears as he approaches the straying band member. Any mare or young horse that ignores the stallion's commands receives a quick bite on its **flank**, the side of a horse between the ribs and the hip, in punishment.

At the first sign of danger—such as the sudden appearance of a person—the stallion snorts a loud alarm and signals for his band to retreat. As his mares and offspring flee, the band stallion lags behind to protect them and to hurry along any band members trailing the rest of the group. He also stops frequently and turns around to face the threat. Then he repeats his loud snorts of warning to both the enemy and his running band.

Each mare in a family band has her own position in the group. This position is recognized by all the other horses. During the escape from an enemy, the most dominant female leads the band while the stallion follows. It is this experienced mare's responsibility to choose the quickest safe route of escape for all the horses. Since at this dangerous time she is the band's leader, she is called the **lead mare**.

Despite the horses' fear during an escape, there is no confusion among the other females following the lead mare. Each mare runs in her proper position with her foal keeping close to her tail. Because every horse knows its place in the band, a retreat is fast and orderly.

A mare's position among the other band members is clear at other times as well. When visiting a small water hole, for example, the dominant mares and their offspring get to drink first. While growing up, young **fillies** (female horses under the age of four) seem to learn their own places in wild horse society by copying the behavior of their mothers. A filly of a dominant mare is likely to become dominant herself when she is older.

The breeding season for mustangs is in late spring, and most foals are born 11 months later in April or May. This is the best time for wild mares to give birth because the cold weather is over, new grass is sprouting, and the foals have the whole summer to grow strong before the next winter arrives.

Band stallions let their mares leave the family band for a day or two to give birth. This is the only time a wild mare leaves the band. Most wild foals are born at night. The darkness of night helps to hide the vulnerable foal. By the morning after its birth, a foal is strong enough to follow its mother back to the family band.

During their first days of life, foals feed on their mother's milk several times each hour. By three or four weeks of age, young horses begin to nibble regularly on the tender spring grass and nurse less often. Foals grow rapidly during their first few months but still tire easily. If the family band must run for a long distance from danger, foals may fall behind. To protect his mares, the band stallion might force the mother of a tiring foal to abandon her offspring. The foal may be left behind so that all the other horses can escape safely. This may sound cruel, but in the wilderness, only the strong and healthy can survive.

By the time they are a year old, young wild horses no longer need their mothers' milk. If a **yearling**, or year old, filly is still with her family band when she is ready to breed for the first time, the band stallion will chase his daughter away to join another stallion's band. Colts, however, are allowed to stay with the family band until they are two or three years old. Then their fathers force them to leave.

Older colts that have been driven from a family band do not live alone, however. There is a second wild horse social group called the **bachelor band**. Older colts that have left their parents' band, and young stallions still unable to win mares make up these bachelor bands. Bachelor groups are composed of two to a dozen young male horses.

Most young stallions take part in lively bouts of play throughout the day. One horse begins by nibbling at another's mouth or chewing and tugging at a companion's mane. This playful activity soon gives way to movements that look much like fighting, but their "battle" is not really serious. Their movements are much slower than in a real stallion fight. The young stallions are careful not to raise their sharp hooves while rearing. Their bites are only gentle nips, and their kicks fall short of touching the companion's hide. Neither horse is injured. This play of young stallions is sometimes called **mock fighting** because it is a pretend battle. Mock fighting gives young stallions the skills they will need to fight successfully for mares.

Most of the time young stallions roaming with a bachelor band enjoy an easy, carefree life. Grazing and playing, galloping to a water hole on a hot afternoon, and then dozing together with his band members after rolling in the cool mud—that's a young stallion's day. Someday the serious business of protecting a harem will leave no time for such relaxation.

One young stallion in each bachelor band acts as the leader. He leads the group in following along behind family bands. Sometimes he even challenges the powerful band stallions. However, a bachelor band's leader almost always retreats without a fight soon after a family band stallion comes forward to face him.

Wild stallions avoid most possible battles and bloodshed by using **ritual posturing** to decide which male is the most dominant. Two stallions stand motionless with their heads together. They breathe heavily into each other's nostrils. Then suddenly, both horses toss their heads and utter loud, furious squeals at the same instant. Often they paw the ground viciously with their front hooves or lash out their hind legs. They may test each other in this way several times before the ritual is ended. When one of the horses finally trots away, the remaining stallion has proved himself the most dominant.

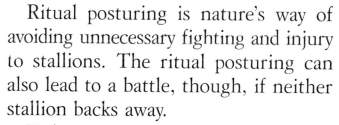

Ritual posturing is nature's way of avoiding unnecessary fighting and injury to stallions. The ritual posturing can also lead to a battle, though, if neither stallion backs away.

Fighting stallions move with surprising speed. They stir up a thick cloud of dust that often hides their battle. Through the dust screen come the sounds of the furious struggle—angry screams, the pounding of hooves, and the thumps of kicks landing against horsehide.

Most mustang battles are short, lasting less than a minute and ending in a draw. The stallions may suffer many bites and hoof cuts, but serious injuries such as broken bones are rare. During the fighting, the family bands wait calmly nearby. Seeming to ignore the battle, the mares go on grazing.

A fight will almost certainly result from an outside stallion's attempt to steal mares from a family band. Some young stallions work together to capture their first mares. When a pair of bachelors approaches a family band, one of the young males will meet the band stallion for ritual posturing and then begin a fight. The second young stallion then steals a mare while his companion and the family band stallion are battling. In this way two young stallions are able to take a mare when neither horse would be able to defeat an older and experienced family band stallion alone.

This behavior may also explain why some family bands have two stallions. They could be young stallion compan-

ions that captured mares together and have not yet separated to form their own individual family bands. Neither stallion is strong enough to chase the other away, but usually only one of them is dominant. The two males watch each other constantly. The dominant stallion always keeps closest to the mares, warning the second stallion away if he comes too near. A fight is likely at any moment between two stallions in the same band.

The third wild horse social group is the **herd**. It is formed when many bands gather together in areas with good grazing and water. Once cowboys watched great herds of thousands of mustangs cross the prairies. Today, because there are far fewer wild horses, the largest herds number from 60 to 150 horses.

Herds can form only when many bands live in the same area because not every band will join a herd. Some family band stallions prefer to keep their harems out of sight from rival males. Large herds can be seen in southern Wyoming and Nevada. Today, the largest wild horse herds are found in the remote Owyhee Desert of northern Nevada.

A herd is made up mostly of family bands, along with a few bachelor bands that stay on the outskirts. Each family band stallion keeps his own mares bunched together and separated from the other harems in the herd. If two family bands drift too close together while grazing, the band stallions prance out to meet each other and perform the ritual posturing. Then they return to their own mares, and both stallions quickly drive their bands farther apart.

When bachelor stallions try to wander among the family bands, the dominant males chase them back to the edge of the herd. There is always tension between the stallions in a herd.

When mustang herds travel to water or fresh pasture, they either walk or trot in single file. Each band follows close behind the next band, so the herd moves in a long string. On their daily trips to a water hole—which may be five or more miles away—the horses wear narrow, winding trails in the dust and sand. They move quietly except for the muffled clumping of their hooves and occasional whiffling sounds as they blow dust from their nostrils.

Herd sizes are not as constant as the sizes of family or bachelor bands. At any time, new horses may join the herd, and other horses may leave it. Or the whole herd may break up one day and the bands scatter. Only the horses know why this is so. A large herd may be sighted grazing on a particular mustang range for weeks or months. Then the horses can disappear overnight.

Wild horses come in many colors and patterns of colors. A herd may contain a great variety of horse colors.

Bay (reddish brown with black mane, tail, and lower legs) is the most common color. Black horses and sorrel

and gray horses are seen more often than palominos (gold-colored horses with white manes and tails) and buckskins (yellowish gray-colored horses). Pintos (which have black or brown coats with patches of white) outnumber Appaloosas (which have a white area on the rump with small dark spots).

Sometimes a wild horse has a black stripe running along its back from mane to tail. Some horses also have faint zebralike stripes on their legs and shoulders. These are primitive markings that reveal the faint traces of Spanish ancestry remaining in some of today's mustangs.

(yellowish brown) horses are also numerous. Roan (a solid-colored horse with white hairs sprinkled through its coat)

The variety of mustang colors and markings are easy to see in a large group of mustangs. A good place to see such a gathering and also to observe mustang behavior is at a water hole. A stallion comes to the water first, checking the area for any danger. Then the rest of the band joins him. Some horses wade into the water to drink. Others stay at the edge of the water hole.

Some horses like to roll in the mud or take a short swim if the water is deep enough, even if the weather is not hot. **Dusting** is another favorite activity following a long drink. After rolling on

the ground, a horse stands and shakes the dust from its hide. Dust baths help keep a mustang's coat in good condition by removing skin oil and loose skin and hair. The ground surrounding a desert pond visited by wild horses is usually worn bare by their dusting.

Young stallions like to practice mock fighting on the bare ground around a water hole. When a family band arrives at water, however, the dominant stallion quickly chases away any young males. When two family bands meet at a water hole, there may be trouble between the two powerful band stallions.

Most often, the family band stallions only test each other with ritual posturing. They breathe nostril to nostril, utter loud squeals, then prance apart to drink with their own mares. Sometimes, however, a furious battle begins in an instant, without any of the normal ritual posturing.

A band stallion must fight many battles in his life to defend his harem. His hide will become rough with scars from the many bites and kicks he receives over the years. Finally he will become too old to protect his band, or he may be crippled by a serious injury. A young challenger will eventually defeat him and win his mares. Then the old, battle-scarred stallion will wander away from the herd to live his last years alone.

Younger stallions will continue to become the new leaders of wild horse bands. Their foals will grow up to be the next generation of mustangs—horses strong and adaptable enough to go on surviving in the American West.

GLOSSARY

bachelor band: a group in mustang society made up of two to a dozen older colts and young stallions

band stallion: the male horse that leads and protects the family band

breed: a group of horses that descends from common ancestors and has similar characteristics

colt: a male horse under four years old

dominant stallion: another name for band stallion

dusting: an activity in which a horse rolls on the ground to remove skin oil and loose skin and hair from its coat

family band: a group in mustang society made up of a band stallion and his harem

filly: a female horse under four years old

foal: a newborn male or female horse

flank: the side of a horse between the ribs and the hip

harem: the female horses in a family band

interbreed: mating of a male and female horse of different breeds

lead mare: the most dominant female horse of a family band

mare: a female horse more than four years old

mock fighting: an activity in which young stallions imitate the movements of a real fight

mustang: horses living in the wild that are descended from different domestic breeds

ritual posturing: a test of dominance between two stallions in which fighting movements are used but no contact is made

stallion: a male horse more than four years old

yearling: a male or female horse that is one year old

herd: a group in mustang society made up of several family bands and a few bachelor bands

hybrid: an offspring of two animals or plants of different breeds

47

ABOUT THE AUTHOR

Jay Featherly grew up in Wyoming and has had a keen interest in wildlife since childhood. He began taking pictures of animals with a box camera when he was ten years old. Currently he photographs and writes about nature professionally. Swans and wild horses have been his most recent animal subjects. *Mustangs: Wild Horses of the American West* is his second Carolrhoda Nature Watch Book.